AF599316

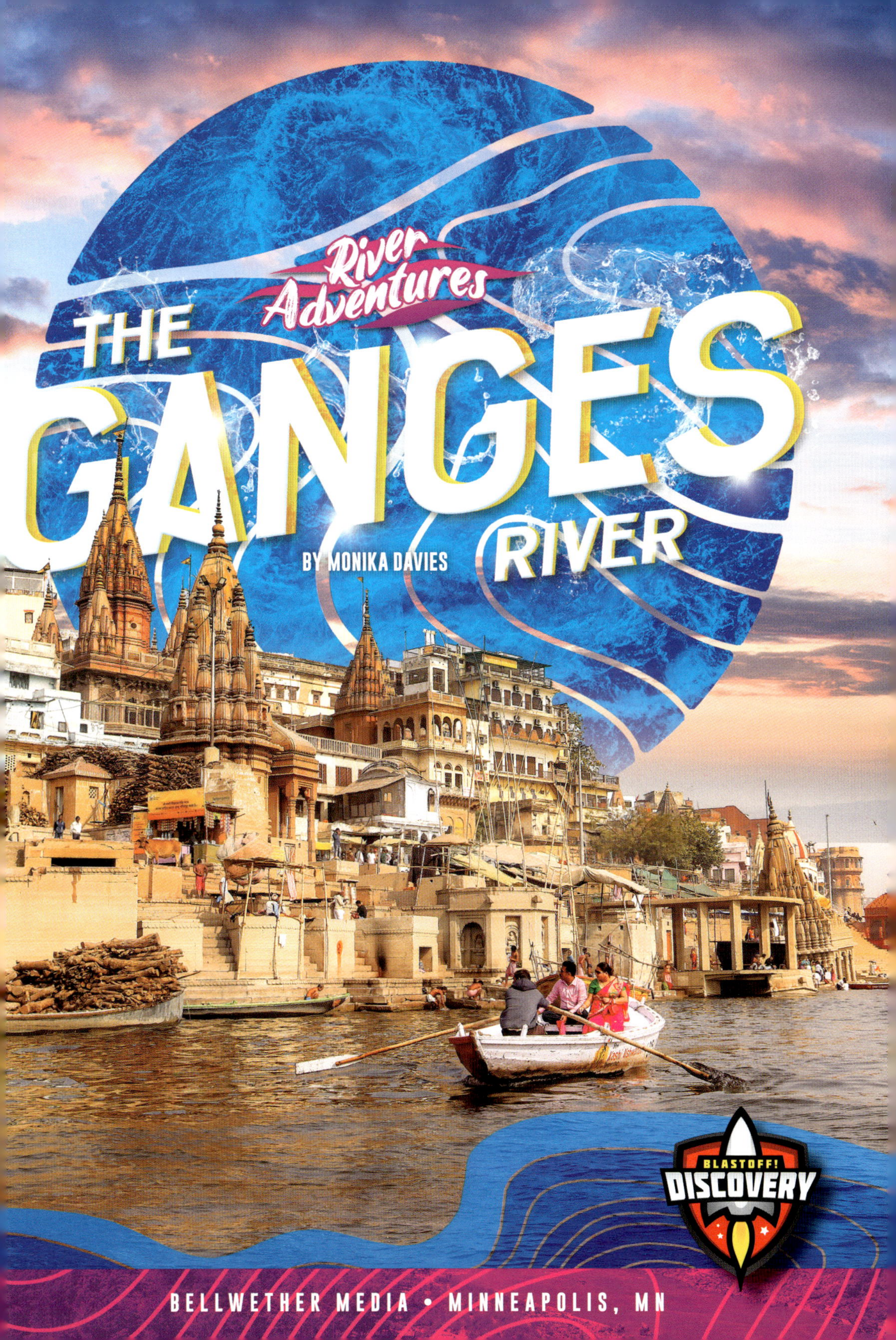
River Adventures
THE GANGES RIVER
BY MONIKA DAVIES
BLASTOFF! DISCOVERY
BELLWETHER MEDIA • MINNEAPOLIS, MN

This edition first published in 2025 by Bellwether Media, Inc.

Library of Congress Cataloging-in-Publication Data

Names: Davies, Monika, author.
Title: The Ganges River / by Monika Davies.
Description: Minneapolis, MN : Bellwether Media,Inc. 2025. | Series: Blastoff! Discovery: River Adventures | Includes bibliographical references and index. | Audience: Ages 7-13 | Audience: Grades 4-6 | Summary: "Engaging images accompany information about the Ganges River. The combination of high-interest subject matter and narrative text is intended for students in grades 3 through 8"- Provided by publisher.
Identifiers: LCCN 2024016548 (print) | LCCN 2024016549 (ebook) | ISBN 9798886879988 (library binding) | ISBN 9781644879306 (ebook)
Subjects: LCSH: Ganges River (India and Bangladesh)-Juvenile literature. | Ganges River Valley (India and Bangladesh)-Juvenile literature.
Classification: LCC DS485.G25 D38 2025 (print) | LCC DS485.G25 (ebook) | DDC 915.4/1-dc23/eng/20240412
LC record available at https://lccn.loc.gov/2024016548
LC ebook record available at https://lccn.loc.gov/2024016549

Editor: Rachael Barnes Designer: Brittany McIntosh

Printed in the United States of America, North Mankato, MN.

TABLE OF CONTENTS

A HOLY RIVER

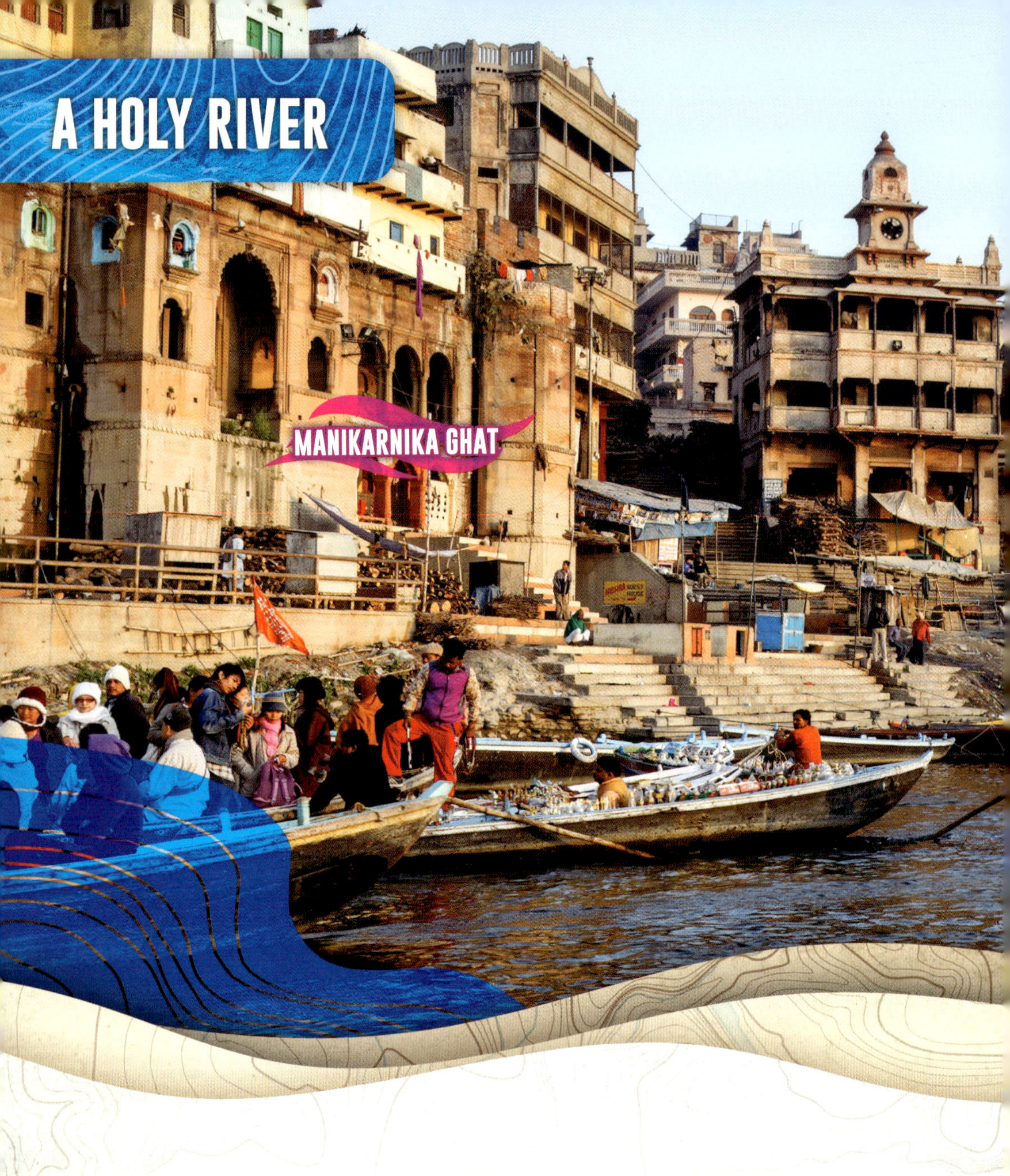

The air is gray and smoky over the Ganges River. The water laps at the base of Manikarnika **Ghat** in Varanasi, India. A religious **ritual** is taking place. Many Hindus are in the holy city to honor loved ones who have died. They believe the Ganges will carry their ashes to heaven.

A RIVER OF MANY NAMES

The Ganges River goes by other names. The river is called Ganga in the Hindi language. Hindu people call the river Mother Ganga.

People walk down the ghat into the river. They pass locals playing instruments on the steps. Some people dip their feet in the water, while others wade to their waist. Many watch the rituals from wooden boats. People have come from all corners of India to experience this holy river.

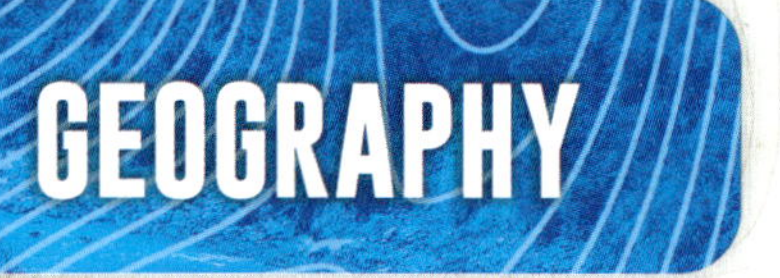

GEOGRAPHY

The Ganges River begins in the Great Himalayas near India's border with Tibet. Its **source** is called Gaumukh. This ice cave is found at the melting tip of Gangotri **Glacier**. Cold, clear water flows from Gaumukh down the mountains.

The glacier water forms the Bhagirathi River. It flows southeast, combining with other **tributaries**. The Bhagirathi meets the Alaknanda River near the city of Devprayag. This **confluence** becomes the Ganges River.

COW'S MOUTH?

Gaumukh means "cow's mouth" in Hindi! The source of the Ganges is named after the unusual shape of the ice cave at its entrance.

The Ganges winds down through the tall peaks of the Himalayas. It flows around a series of foothills. The river continues into the Indo-Gangetic **Plain**. It moves slowly across northern India. Farther on, the Yamuna River merges with the Ganges. This tributary joins the Ganges in Prayagraj, India.

HIMALAYAS

The river turns south as it enters Bangladesh. The Brahmaputra River meets the Ganges to form an expansive **delta**. This region of **mangrove forests** and swamps is called the Sundarbans. The Ganges then empties into the Bay of Bengal.

FLOODING IN BANGLADESH

A MIGHTY RIVER SYSTEM

The Ganges River is about 1,560 miles (2,511 kilometers) long. The river basin is over 419,000 square miles (1,085,205 square kilometers). It is one of the largest river systems in the world!

The Ganges River changes throughout the year. The river's usual slow pace gains speed and force when **monsoons** hit from July to October. These winds bring heavy rain that often causes damaging floods in the delta. Dangerous **cyclones** may start in the Bay of Bengal at the beginning and end of the monsoon season.

The seasonal rainfall and melting glacier ice change the river's depth. The western end of the river **basin** receives around 30 inches (76 centimeters) of rain each year. The eastern end gets up to 90 inches (229 centimeters) of rain.

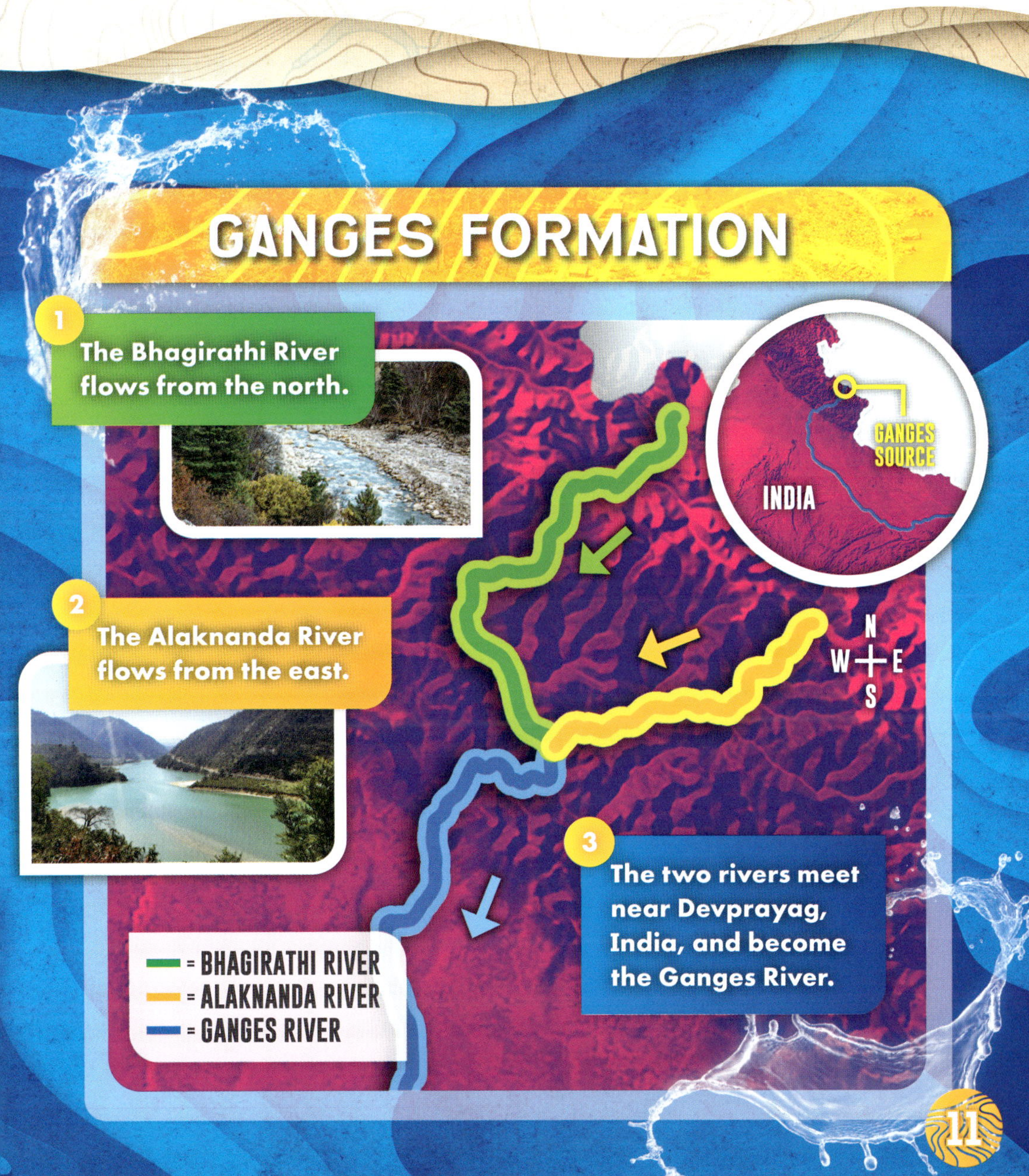

PLANTS AND ANIMALS

Thick forests used to surround the Ganges River. Now, most of the land near the river is used for farming. This has changed which plants and animals live in or near the Ganges. Chital and wild boars roam the Indo-Gangetic Plain near the river. Indian softshell turtles lay eggs near the water's edge.

Ganges river dolphins dip and dive through the river. They use sound to hunt shrimp and small fish. River lapwings and Indian skimmers fly overhead.

CHITAL

WILD BOAR

INDIAN SOFTSHELL TURTLE

INDIAN SKIMMER

RIVER LAPWING

GANGES RIVER DOLPHIN
Life Span: up to 30 years
Status: endangered
Ganges river dolphin range =
LEAST CONCERN
NEAR THREATENED
VULNERABLE
ENDANGERED
CRITICALLY ENDANGERED
EXTINCT IN THE WILD
EXTINCT

The Ganges River delta is the largest in the world. Birds rest on the delta when winter comes. Ducks, terns, and storks flock to the waters.

FAMOUS SIGHTS

Around 250 different types of birds flock to the Sundarbans. The region is also known for having the world's largest population of Bengal tigers.

PURPLE HERON

BENGAL TIGER

Many animals are protected in Sundarban National Park. Bengal tigers prowl for deer and wild boars among the trees. Otters sunbathe along the river. Gharials and crocodiles watch nearby. Carps and barbs swim underwater. Black-capped kingfishers cackle in the trees while purple herons pick their way through grasses and reeds. Asian openbills slowly wade through the shallow swamp.

HUMAN HISTORY

The Ganges River has flowed quietly through many chapters of human history. Centuries ago, the Vedic people moved to the Indo-Gangetic Plain. The Vedic people began as **nomads**. In time, they began to build villages. They used the river to grow crops on the western Ganges plain.

Later, different groups of people fought to control the Ganges River. The Magadha kingdom eventually won. The kingdom established its capital on the Ganges in what is now the city of Patna, India.

VEDISM

The religion of the Vedic people was called Vedism. Hinduism grew out of Vedism.

MAURYAN RUINS

Over the centuries, many **dynasties** and **empires** rose and fell on the Indo-Gangetic Plain. Powerful rulers chose to center their empires along the Ganges. The Mauryan Empire once controlled much of present-day India. The center of the empire was near today's Patna. It relied on the river and its access to the Bay of Bengal for trade.

Three dynasties fought over the Indo-Gangetic Plain in the 8th century. Each dynasty wanted control over which ships were allowed to travel the river. The ruling dynasty could also access nearby trees and sandstone to use as building materials.

GANGES RIVER TIMELINE

1200 BCE
Vedic people begin to build villages in the western plain near the Ganges

AROUND 321 BCE
The Mauryan Empire is founded, often using the river and the Bay of Bengal for trade routes

1750 CE
Ramnagar Fort is built along the Ganges near the city of Varanasi

1975
The Farakka Barrage opens on the Ganges

2023
The Namami Gange Mission II is confirmed, adding $2.56 billion to a project to help keep the Ganges River clean

Multiple cities and landmarks rose along the river. In Haridwar, India, the holy Har Ki Pauri ghat was built next to the river in the 1st century BCE. Hundreds of ghats and temples were made along the Ganges in Varanasi.

CULTURAL CONNECTION

KUMBH MELA

WHAT IS IT?

A weeks-long Hindu festival held every four years

WHERE IS IT?

A religious site along the Ganges or another sacred river in India

FESTIVAL SIZE

Millions of people, making it the largest peaceful gathering of humanity on Earth

FUN FACT

Gatherings for this purpose have been recorded since as early as 629 CE

Powerful groups continued to live near the Ganges. They built forts to control the river. Ramnagar Fort, built in 1750 CE, still stands on the river near Varanasi. Later, dams were built along the river to control the flow of the Ganges. The Indian government built the Farakka Barrage dam in 1975. It directs river water back into India toward Kolkata.

THE RIVER TODAY

KOLKATA

The Ganges River basin is home to over 650 million people. People in this area depend on the river for food, fresh water, and work. Crops like rice and sugarcane grow in the rich soil along the river. The Ganges is used to water these crops. People also fish in the river.

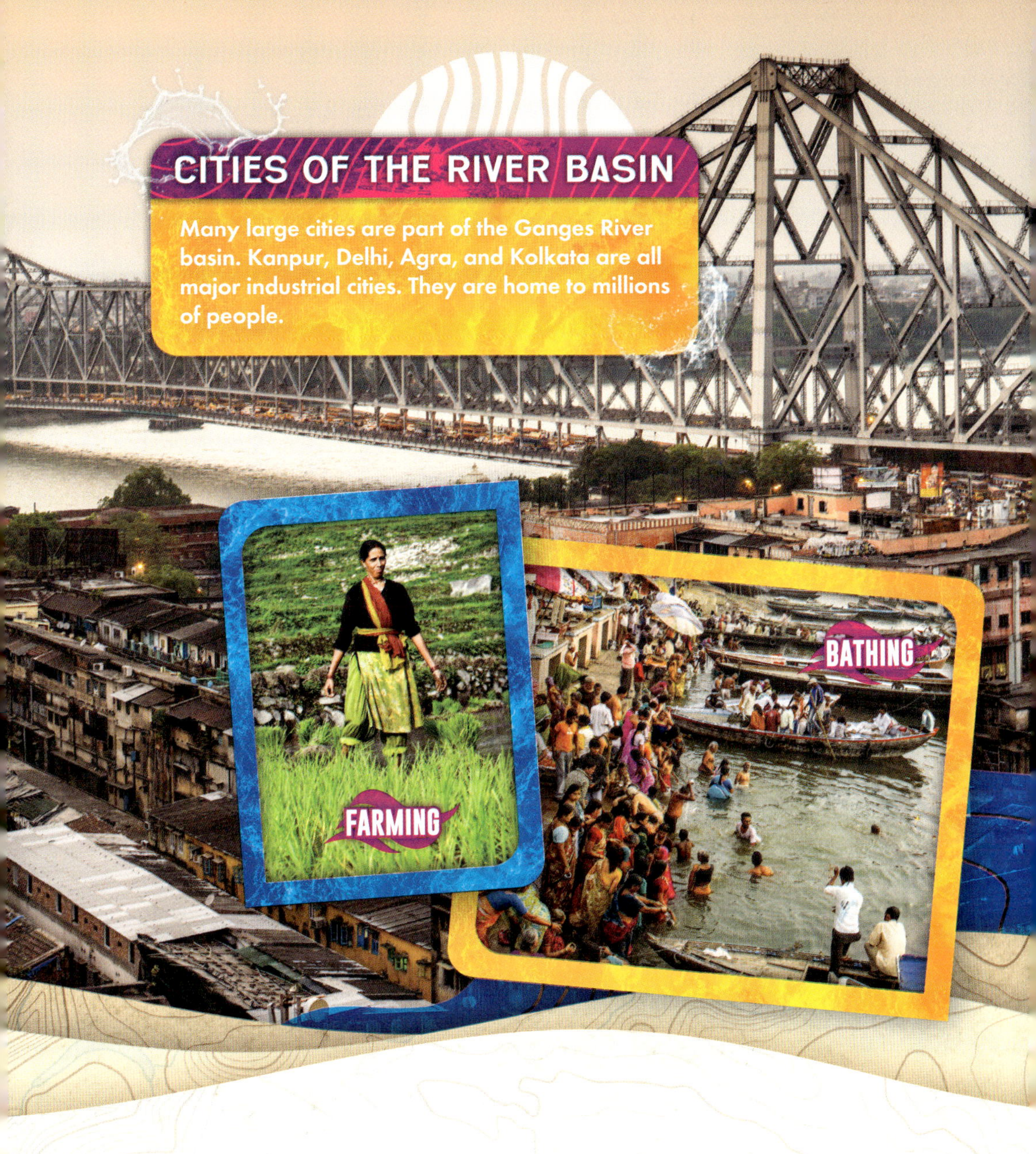

The Ganges is the most **sacred** river for Hindus. They come to the Ganges for holy rituals. They bathe in the river. They spread the ashes of their loved ones over the water. Millions of people celebrate religious festivals along the river.

RIVER PROJECT PROFILE

TEHRI DAM

WHAT IS IT?

A dam on the Bhagirathi River

OPENED

2006

PURPOSE

Built to store and gather water for drinking, electricity, and farming

Cities along the Ganges have added many structures to the river. There are now hundreds of dams in the Ganges River basin. Many of the dams in India are used for **hydropower**. They create electricity for the nation. The Tehri Dam is one of the largest.

The dams in India, including the Farakka Barrage, prevent much of the Ganges's waters from reaching Bangladesh. This harms Bangladesh's farming and fishing **industries**. It also makes floods and **droughts** more severe. The two countries continue to fight over the Ganges River's water supply today.

PROTECTING THE RIVER

The Ganges River is facing major threats. Over time, **climate change** has altered the river's flow. The glaciers that add to the river are shrinking. During the dry season, the river sometimes does not even meet the Bay of Bengal.

Pollution is obvious in much of the Ganges. Many cities and towns drain untreated human waste directly into the river. Factories dump waste into the water. Some Hindu rituals can add pollution to the water, too. Ashes and flower offerings clog the Ganges. The flowers are often treated with chemicals that are harmful to the river and its wildlife.

SEVERE DRY SEASON

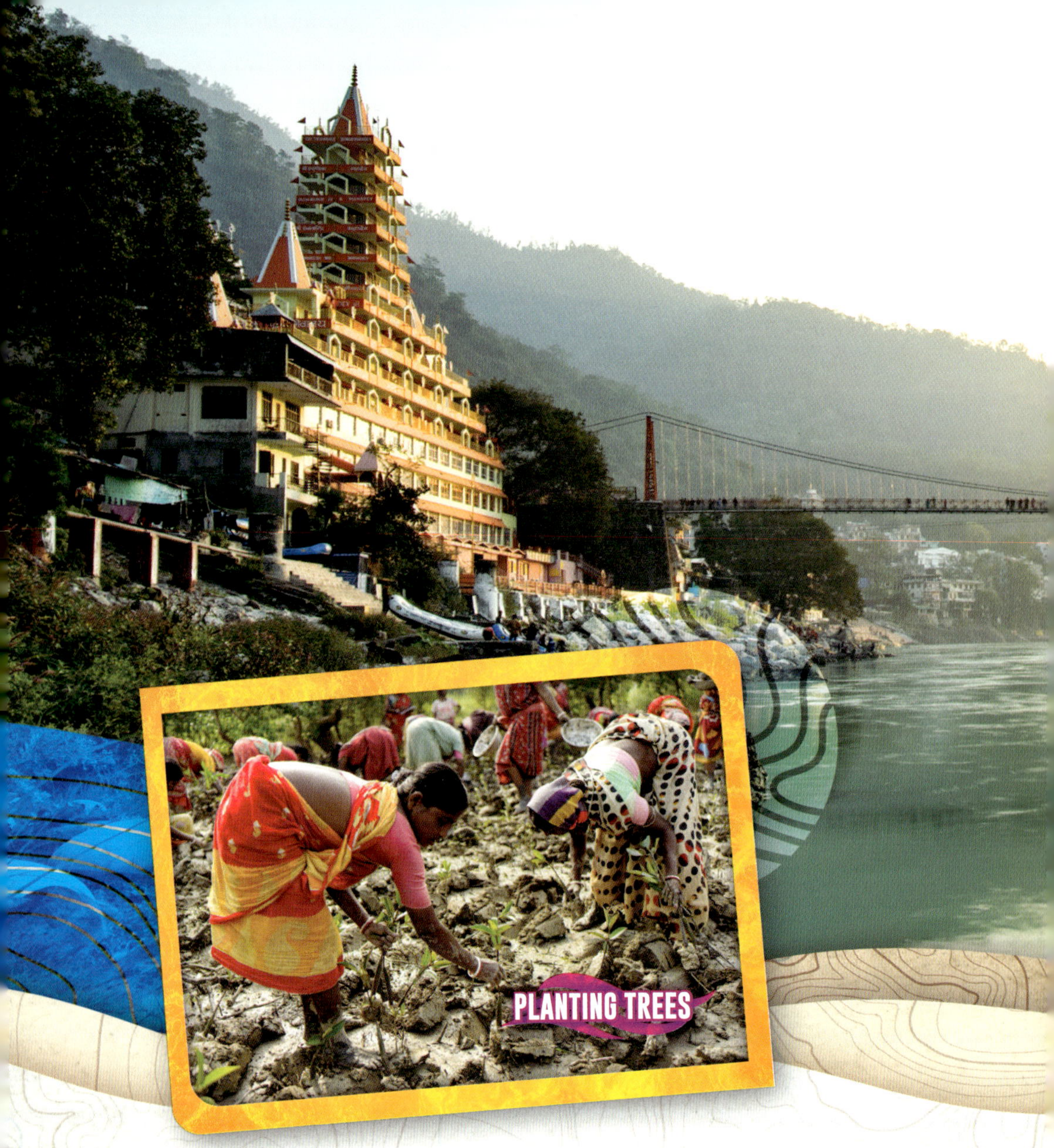

PLANTING TREES

The Indian government has several action plans to help the Ganges River. They plan to plant trees along the river. Their 2030 target is to cover 521 square miles (1,349 kilometers) of land near the river in forests. The trees can keep pollution out of the river.

The Namami Gange Programme is another government program. It aims to build better systems in cities so less human waste ends up in the river. People all over the river basin are learning how to care for the water. The Ganges has a challenging future, but many are committed to cleaning up this treasured river.

GLOSSARY

basin—the area drained by a river

climate change—a human-caused change in Earth's weather due to warming temperatures

confluence—the place where two rivers meet

cyclones—storms with high winds that often bring a lot of rain

delta—a land area that forms where a river flows into a large body of water

droughts—long periods of dry weather

dynasties—lines of rulers that come from the same family

empires—groups of people led by one ruler

ghat—a flight of steps leading down to an Indian river

glacier—a massive sheet of ice that covers a large area of land

hydropower—the energy created by moving water

industries—types of businesses that make a particular good or perform a specific service

mangrove forests—thick tropical forests that can grow along coasts in salty swamp water

monsoons—winds that shift direction each season; monsoons bring heavy rain.

nomads—people who have no fixed home but wander from place to place

plain—a large area of flat land

ritual—a religious ceremony or practice

sacred—relating to religion

source—the beginning of a river

tributaries—rivers and streams that flow into a larger stream, river, or lake

TO LEARN MORE

AT THE LIBRARY

DK. *Illustrated Atlas of India*. New York, N.Y.: DK Publishing, 2020.

Green, Sara. *Ancient India*. Minneapolis, Minn.: Bellwether Media, 2020.

Harris, Tim. *Wildlife Worlds Asia*. New York, N.Y.: Crabtree Publishing Company, 2020.

ON THE WEB

FACTSURFER

Factsurfer.com gives you a safe, fun way to find more information.

1. Go to www.factsurfer.com.

2. Enter "Ganges River" into the search box and click 🔍.

3. Select your book cover to see a list of related content.

INDEX

The images in this book are reproduced through the courtesy of: Roop Dey/ Alamy, front cover; apple2499, p. 3; Graham Prentice/ Alamy, pp. 4-5; CherylRamalho, p. 5 (inset); SauravRawat, pp. 6-7, 8 (top); Vasily Gureev, p. 7 (inset); Steve Photography, p. 8 (bottom); Azzu fashion, p. 9; NurPhoto SRL/ Alamy, p. 10; Rudolf Thalhammer, p. 11 (top); jeygupt, p. 11 (bottom); Sriram Bird Photographer, p. 12 (Indian skimmer); Travel Stock, p. 12 (chital); WildMedia, p. 12 (wild boar); kunaljain7, p. 12 (Indian softshell turtle); Butterfly Hunter, p. 12 (river lapwing); Binoy B Gogoi, p. 13; Rich Lindie, p. 14 (gharial); Andyworks/ iStockphoto, p. 14 (purple heron); Naveen Kallur, p. 14 (Bengal tiger); Wojtkowski Cezary/ Alamy, p. 15; Radiokukka/ iStockphoto, p. 16; explorewithinfo, pp. 16-17; Paulose NK, p. 18; deepak bishnoi, p. 19 (top); AnilD, p. 19 (middle); Md Alfaj Alam, p. 19 (bottom); Luisa Puccini, p. 20; cornfield, p. 21 (top); Krishna8412, p. 21 (bottom); Mazur Travel, pp. 22-23, 23 (right); Kettik Images/ Alamy, p. 23 (left); valdiya_ravi, p. 24; Majority World CIC/ Alamy, p. 25; Pacific Press/ Contributor/ Getty Images, p. 26; Doctors photography, pp. 26-27; SOPA Images Limited/ Alamy, p. 28; travelwild, pp. 28-29; RAHUL_BRAHMA, p. 31.